Double Helix

poems by

Robin Dellabough

Finishing Line Press
Georgetown, Kentucky

Double Helix

Copyright © 2022 by Robin Dellabough
ISBN 978-1-64662-844-5 First Edition
All rights reserved under International and Pan-American Copyright Conventions. No part of this book may be reproduced in any manner whatsoever without written permission from the publisher, except in the case of brief quotations embodied in critical articles and reviews.

Publisher: Leah Huete de Maines

Editor: Christen Kincaid

Cover Art: Marlitt Dellabough

Author Photo: Alhy Berry

Cover Design: Marlitt Dellabough

Order online: www.finishinglinepress.com
also available on amazon.com

Author inquiries and mail orders:
Finishing Line Press
P. O. Box 1626
Georgetown, Kentucky 40324
U. S. A.

Table of Contents

Part One
Affliction (1) 1
For Sale: Black Metal File Cabinet 2
The Eighth Year 4
Going Away 5
First Night in Amagansett 6
Last Days in Amagansett 7
After Thirty Years 8
Trapeze Lesson 9
After Image 10
The Velocity of Nostalgia 11
Natural History: *Apis mellifera* 12
Parting Shots 13
Instructions for Letting Go of a Marriage 14
Topsy-turvy 16
Separation 17
What's the Worst That Can Happen? 19
Bitter 20
Dwelling 21
Affliction (2) 22

Part Two
Furtive Hours 25
This World 26
My Boy 27
Quieten 28
Beach Lessons 29
Reproduction 30
Good Friday 31
Serenity 32
Leather 33
Crossing 34
Dioscuri 35
Chado 36
Almost Nowhere 37
How I Say God 38

Samsara 39
New York City Police Report #953 40
Supplication 41
My Son's Birthday 42

Part Three
How To Be Born Twice 47
Unsheltered 48
Undone 49
Double Helix 50
Incarnations 51
Origin Story 52
First Father Speaks 53
Second Father Speaks 54
Hegira 55
Hecate Incarnate 56
Warren 57
Recall 59
February 4 60
Names 61
Chiromancy 62
Last Spring 63
Call and Response Double Sonnet 64
Water Lilies 65
The Dog Eats A Letter From My Mother When I Was 18 66
Rigging 68
Making Sense 69
Before And After Kennedy 70
Affliction (3) 71
Exposure 72
I Find A Haiku Written 36 Years Before My DNA Test 73
Affliction (4) 74
Collaboration 75
Family Dinner, 1976 77

Acknowledgments 79
About the Author 81

For Dorothy Nelson Dellabough
my first poet

Part One

Affliction (1)

The year I was afflicted with love,
we took my parents to Windows on the World
to toast our oblivious happiness with Veuve Clicquot,

while we looked out toward the future
and down past any fear of heights,
then skipped past fountains to One If By Land,

where I wasn't even bored as the men
rattled on about American wars
and we ate Beef Wellington in front of a fire.

Now both marriages and that iconic building
have burned into history but new architecture soars
and love still bears witness with new lives, alive, a life.

For Sale: Black Metal File Cabinet

Do you need to save this?
Official receipt of County Clerk of Alameda County
September 2, 1981 fee for filing marriage
Absolutely not.

Or this?
Certificate of Live Birth June 24, 1983
No, he loses it at least once a year.
Then keep it.
What if he dies?
You'll know he was alive.

Weil-McClain Cast Iron Boiler limited warranty
Fender guitar receipt
I forgot about that guitar.
You don't remember his lessons up in the attic?
No, I only remember him rummaging late at night.

Joint 2000 tax return, Roper and Lark
Did we make enough?
Enough to go to Paris that year. All of us.

Passport cancelled April 12, 2005
Therapy bills: adjustment disorder with anxious mood
Is that why we divorced?
Maybe. I'm still anxious.

Scarsdale Eye Center June 10, 2007
Or your fear of glaucoma? You haven't gone blind yet.
No, but I don't see clearly.

Northwest Mutual Life Insurance policy, 2011
I think I'm the only beneficiary.
Do you wish me dead? Do you wish I were dead?

So many pounds of paper.
Do you feel lighter?
I do feel lighter.

How light?
Well, not untethered.
Not untethered. But lighter.
Light and tethered.
Tethered to what?
Still wanting to be tethered. Light.

The Eighth Year

In the outback of Australia,
    after eight drought years,
    it rained.
Survivors covered in mud shouted
    their faith in the rain,
    a wet religion,
while the earth, dry but never barren,
    revealed buried seeds
    rushing up
    toward water.

After our dry quiet days,
    when we come
    together
    again, rushing
    toward tears
until we are drenched,
we live on what grows,
    sustained
through the next drought,
    not by hope
    or even love,
but by the inevitability of rain.

Going Away

On the road, we got stuck in our familiar loop,
the endless same-old, like bickering children.

Once we were there, we lay in the dark,
recounting miseries, stroking them like worry beads,

even as you touched my open back,
even as we almost made another child.

                    Later, too hot to sleep,
swaying and sweating all night

until we exchanged dreams: China, bicycles,
a river, doughnuts, Phoenix.

Now, sitting on the edge of glossy morning,
I know that when your dreams find a way

inside my poems, we are married
and married again.

First Night in Amagansett

We find our way to the ocean's dark edge.
I shine a flashlight straight up,
a beam to make a path in sky.

He says *Don't do that,*
you could blind a pilot.

I laugh. Surrounded by amber moon sliver,
glowing white wave crests, evocative bonfire,
how could anyone be blind?

But I don't see the two shooting stars
that fall across his field of vision.

Last Days in Amagansett

The past was sometimes tense
with yearning for our future:

We'd swim close to each other,
never too far from shore.

We'd see everyone else we loved
standing on their own.

We were safe and free
together in our watery garden,

grown out of tears and kisses
we can't take back.

After Thirty Years

He says *You were a good mother.*
You need therapy.
You wear a tragic mask.

He says *You have a nice body.*
You always judge me.
You told me what to do.

He says *You read novels.*
You are competent.
You are older than me.

He says *I need a break.*

I say *Fuck you.*

Trapeze Lesson

When he moves out, I take off my ring.
It feels naked and momentous,
until I remember one other time.

I climbed the ladder easily to swing out
fast, between the city and the river,
not knowing what the hardest part would be:

letting go, letting go, letting go.

After Image

Remember that first May here?
Through the tunnel into thick wet green,
a tiny tribe foraging for connection.
At dusk I'd wait on the front steps,
watching our son and daughter light up,
their arms like sturdy wings
as they stirred still air.
I'd wait for you to walk from the river
back to us, all of us, our green.

This May you are in a different green,
while I wait again, seeing
the after image of that first spring,
those children running back to me.

The Velocity of Nostalgia

How lovely that Barnum's animal crackers
still come in the little orange box like a train car,
that Hudson Line conductors still take tickets,
the same way they took John Cheever's back
when the train had a bar.

Now you have to get house white
to go in a plastic cup that always leaks
from the Taste of New York shop in Grand Central,
where the funny counter guy just died.
His daughter owns One Woman winery,
which still uses corks. Some might say screw
tops are an improvement but corks force

you to slow down,

maybe catch a later train,

to remember riding home

to a family playing Monopoly at dusk,

while a bouquet of bicycles

twirled down the street.

You can never catch up but you can adore from any distance.

Natural History: *Apis mellifera*

When you left me
it was like leaving a hive open in August,

honeycomb full, a sweet magnet
for thousands of plundering bees,

sucking out the labor of months in a few hours,
loud as a yellow tunnel,

oblivious in their furious hunger
until all that's left is a wax skeleton,

and the beekeeper saying
You must start again.

You must start again.

Parting Shots

Putting on my favorite top from Anthropologie,
I suddenly remember the worst thing he said
before he left our long marriage. It wasn't
that store is too young for you. Not
you make me feel like the junior partner
or *you read novels and do crosswords.*
It wasn't *your face is a mirror of grief.*
Not even *I'm not sure I ever loved you.*
No, it was that knowing I had lived in a treehouse
in Hawaii, hitchhiked through Europe at seventeen,
written dozens of books, started my own company,
that I am a teacher, a poet, a mother,
knowing all those things, the best he could come up
with was *you're a good housekeeper.*

Instructions for Letting Go of a Marriage

Pick the coldest, windiest day of the year.

Sort through piles of letters, birthday cards, vacation plans, and wedding vows until you're sure he did love you.

Hesitate about whether you can burn this evidence.
Wonder if your kids would ever like to read it.
Decide absolutely not.

Gather matches. Find matchbook from restaurant where you told your parents you were getting married. Decide to burn that too.

Try not to look at dog as you put your coat on.
Decide absolutely not to bring dog with you.

Bring dog to park by river. See large sign: NO DOGS ALLOWED.

Let dog off leash. Watch dog chase geese. Watch dog eat geese shit.

Call dog and tie him up.

Put letters in small BBQ grill. Put rocks on top so they won't blow away.

Take gloves off to light matches. Immediately freeze hands.

Gale winds. Try to light matches. Won't light. Keep trying dozens of matches until only few matches left.

Decide need another approach.

Walk to boat club next door. Find debris. Try to build wind shield.
Doesn't work.

Find large plastic pail. Put letters in bottom. Light match. Wind makes crazy huge flames. Worry going to burn down boat club. Notice dog trying to eat something under dock.

Watch letters burn to ash. Plastic pail has melted too. Find cup to scoop up ashes.

Walk back to park to throw ashes in river. Try not to slip on slippery rocks. Notice all the ashes have already blown out of cup. Laugh out loud.

Start walking home. See only other person in entire park. Next door neighbor. Says a perky hello. Notice she's wondering why carrying empty cup, purse, and dog. Wants to chat. Say need to get out of park due to dog eating geese shit.

Go home. Feed dog. Feed self.

Topsy-turvy

I'm in the basement looking through moldy cardboard boxes for my daughter's old topsy-turvy doll from an Underground Railroad Museum, because my ex-husband wants it for a group of Quakers in Richmond, Indiana but I can't find it. He could probably get one on Ebay so I search online and find dozens of dolls, one head black, the other white, but they aren't for sale. I find articles on their cultural meaning, no doubt little black girls being raised with little white girls in the 19th century played with such dolls. No one is saying if that was okay or not. I think about my granddaughter, Rachel, whose mother is Zulu and whose father is white and wonder what she'd make of such a doll or whether her mother would be offended, and I think Rachel must already feel like a topsy-turvy doll, going back and forth from one parent's house to another's, not looking quite like either one. In the end I decide to tell my ex that he can look for his own damn doll.

Separation

Agreement made this day
    by and between
the "Wife"
    the "Husband"
whereas married
civil   ceremony
diverse disputes and differences
    have arisen
discussed rights, privileges and obligations
    own free will
terms, covenants   and conditions
promises and undertakings

Article 1: Independent Lives
neither shall molest or disturb the peace
    free to act   unmarried
free from interference
    authority   control

Article 11: Real Estate
marital home   encumbered
    equity
Wife indemnify   and hold harmless

Article 111: Equitable Distribution
    joint accounts
implication consents   thereto
    marital personal   property
remove from   marital home
    Wife will retain dog

Article IV: Maintenance
upon remarriage
    upon death
Wife   inform Husband   may benefit
filed joint   all years of their marriage

Article V: Life Insurance
Husband   on his life
      breach   Husband's death
proof   of existence
upon request

Article VI: Dispute Resolution
If a conflict arises
in favor of   noticing party
      defaulting party
obtaining   such relief

In witness whereof
the parties
      have set their hands
and seal
      hereby
dissolved

What's the Worst That Can Happen?

You meet for drinks, pinot gris for you,
pinot noir for him, trade the usual blah-blah
while trying to get a read—a bead?—on each other:

he's tall, you're thin, he's Jewish, you're not,
he's smart, you're smart, it's like inventory
at a human being store. You have buyer's remorse,

reluctant to make such a big purchase again.
Instead you try an installment plan but it stalls
as you squeeze yourselves into calendars

fat with trips, children, doctors, dogs,
baseball games, swing classes, legal conferences—
at this rate, you won't even be holding hands

until next year, and you're impatient to find out
how a new body might fit your old body,
will they click into place like toy magnetic trains

or will his skin grate your skin raw?
Then he says you're off the hook, he's met someone.
Of course you're insulted, yet you want

to be alone with your own words, your ferns,
white peaches on a warm day,
feeling a tiny puff of air like a lover's touch.

What's the worst that can happen?
You end up being the only witness
to your life, and six out of seven days,

you try to believe that's enough.
On the seventh day, it is more than enough.

Bitter

Chestnuts plummet like green bombs.
My brother turns them into liqueur.
A robin slams into glass, ricochets away,
leaving wingprints and one tiny feather.
Bewitched, Bothered and Bewildered
brings sudden tears, another kind of blow.
Did my parents dance to it before I could speak?
Or was it me and my husband,
who now lives with his girlfriend
and their dog named Eros.

I want to wish him happiness. But no.
I want chestnuts and robins to pummel
him senseless until he cries out
and fox trots back to me. But no.

Dwelling

She folds a house from pages
of her divorce decree, cuts out a door,

puts one Peruvian lily, a blue heron
feather, and her wedding ring inside,

then sets it on fire. Their marriage
is in a spirit house now.

Affliction (2)

The year I was afflicted with sudden separation,
I put on a strapless dress because he once loved
those shoulders. I accused him, a master of divinity,
of not being Christian or kind.
I was talking to an empty space, and
separated from myself, had to find
a dry wilderness large enough to shrink loss.
Hiking straight up to Enchantment Lakes,
past bitterroot and bleeding heart,
I scrabbled across granite, following cairns.
Like *Camellia japonica* spreading
its branches low to the ground for protection
from snow, I would not break.

Part Two

Furtive Hours

An elephant sits in the mid-century modern living room,
        waiting for someone to ask *how do you do?*
while someone we love is slipping out a back door
        without saying goodbye. We hear a lock click open
before we realize he's out running with foxes,
        silent burrowers, badgers and snakes,
all those smaller creatures that will harm him
        as we are getting to know the huge gray beast.

This World

At four, he said *I don't want to be in this world.*
My love leapt out of the body that bore him,
hovered over his infant despair, a silent roar
to crack open his heart and let me back in.

At eleven: *I don't fit in this world.*
We flailed and floundered, changed his school,
as he shut himself high in the house
we thought would tether him to tenderness.

At twenty-four: *I won't stay in this world.*
His sister cut him down at 2 a.m.
just before the rope had done its job.
I told him to borrow my hope.

At thirty-five, he comes back from the nearly dead.
His own four-year-old whispers *Daddy's all better,*
and draws concentric hearts. I will blizzard him
with those hearts, until he says *I want to be in this world.*

My Boy

Home again for a moment,
he rests face down in the sun,
his head turned so I can see
his shuttered eyes, the thickened hair
covering his legs until
in one sudden inhalation

he is a man

and I can't ask him certain things,
those questions will have to leave
my body the same way he left
me, coming into this world.

Quieten

A small boy's gone missing
in palm- and rose-lined streets.
Have you seen him? the woman asks.

Later, I hear the boy was hiding
in the lush back garden. I wonder
what made him so angry

he could stay still, hearing
voices frantic with dread
call his name.

I remember another child
who drowned in a backyard pool
because no one heard his cries.

When my son disappeared in aqua water,
I learned what wringing hands meant.
As I waited for him to surface,

I didn't shout. I prayed his name
over and over until he swam around
the rocks to us for a little longer.

Beach Lessons

Waves can be cradles or churning
traps but are relentless.

A tower of skimming clouds
is a relief after days of blue.

Black rectangles speckling the sand
are empty egg purses.

Starfish grow six or seven arms
if they lose one of their original five.

Every child building a castle
builds your child's lost dreams.

When your son says he's in detox again,
you are grateful for salt water.

Reproduction

First, a man and woman fuck.

Yowling like a feral cat, he or she

is not glad to be born.

Still, the man and woman fall in love

with this near replica, its coy smile,

all pink softness concealing so many

varieties of invisible disorder.

It takes years before these nightmares erupt.

By then it's too late to unlove, unattach,

the man and woman must stand apart,

witnesses to what, innocently, they made.

Fuck the whole fucking world

where innocence does not exist.

Good Friday

J stumbles out of a black jeep
onto the rain-soaked grass
holding a half-empty bottle of Koskenkorva.
He wants to stay, just one night.
He cries *I thought you cared about me,*
I'm not a bad person
as he crucifies himself drop by drop.
I water the forsythia with vodka,
maybe it will bloom clear tears.
The empty glass breaks, splinters my eye.
On Easter, J calls from Bellevue,
asks what will happen.
My words turn into glass.

Serenity

After the whirligig of days—

my son lost in sticky toxic tendrils
again and again,

mother lost in thickets of faulty neurons
over and over,

husband lost in his secret shame,
once and for all—

I lose myself in exhausting efforts of hope
until I develop a penchant for clean white tables,

the scent of lemons, a yellow tulip,
air so still I can touch it like a linen bed—

unwaking, unlonging.

Leather

The profligate son hinges down
to a chair made of animal skin,
cracked and scarred. He wishes
he could pull it over himself to make
a home where he'd be painproof,
no need for tiny arrows he keeps close,
a quiver of prickly protection.
He'd be able to sip from a dry cup,
stretch his frayed joints back
to a bamboo trail where he once walked
quiet with contentment, unaffected
by hoarfrost or headwinds.

For now, he imagines the chair again
beating blood, it rears up and canters away.

Crossing

Once a mother and child stood hand in hand
about to cross the simple wooden bridge
over a riffling brook. They took their time.
The mother would stop to point out fallfish,
emerald shiners, or granite rock for her
boy's elation, which dowsed her lightly.

Now the mother is still a mother but
the child is a man on the opposite side
of a tangled, truss-beamed bridge that looms
high above agitated water,
its roar drowning out her voice.
He can't see across to her face, willing
him to throw only his pain off the bridge,
to remember one glinting rock.

Dioscuri

After watching *The Parent Trap*,
my granddaughter sees twins
at the park, on a train,
not sure if they're doubles or halves.

My son dreams of a parallel life
where his flourishing twin
is filled with steadiness,
as whole as two halves.

I imagine that, like generous Pollux,
who sacrificed immortality for his twin
so he and Castor are now stars,
my son's twin will share his health halved.

That would be a gift for weeping
over in wonder, even half,
like the crystal composites whose parts
are reversed in reflection: twinned.

Chado

Remember you said *before I was your little boy
I was an old Chinese man walking
on a narrow path high in the mountains.*
Then you drew a yin yang symbol.

Remember your collection of *chadogu*—
antique tea bowls, shallow for summer cooling,
deep ones to keep tea hot in winter,
chasen in every size, like bamboo sculptures.

Remember that year I flew cross country,
packing it all in a carry-on to surprise you?
It didn't break but you lost everything,
exchanging tea for vodka, *chasen* for needles.

Now you take Metro North each morning
from a shelter in Harlem
to your childhood home on Maple Street,
where packages stamped from Japan arrive.

You weigh 3.2 grams of loose leaf sencha,
then place a strainer over the measuring cup.
Boil filtered water in a kettle
with precise settings: oolong, black, matcha.

Pour over leaves, steep two minutes
according to the timer. Drink pale jade
from white porcelain. Repeat five times
daily, grateful for the way of tea.

Almost Nowhere

On Wilshire Boulevard in front of Erewhon,
the woman wearing white boots in morning fog
repeats *I don't know where I put them*
as she paces near her cart piled with old sneakers,
a fake fur blanket, *National Geographics.*
Her blonde hair, cut short, almost chic, is a mystery:
was it just yesterday her life fissured,
tossing her to the far side of sanity?
Or was it a slow slide from ketamine
to crystal to vodka, rehabs to psych wards,
shelters to sleeping on subways?
I'm not talking about her anymore.
It's my son's birthday. He is somewhere else,
a little alive. I teeter between ending and faith.

How I Say God

When she died, my mother left me with joy,
the angel card I pulled as we stood behind
the Unitarian Church in a circle around her ashes.
My son, already deep into his demons,
was not there. Today he sits in my kitchen,
waiting for a van to take him to his nineteenth
rehab after getting out of his forty-third
detox. His eyes are sunken, no light,
hands shaking. I ask if he'd like to bring
a photo of his daughter, he says no thank you.
Then I pull joy. Each time he says he's tired
or sorry or angry or afraid, I touch the word
as if it were a rosary bead or worry stone:
Joy. Mother. Joy. Make him well. Joy. Joy.

Samsara

He is hollowed out.
The white of one eye is blood-filled.
He has a bitter smell so I drench him
in sweet syrup but he dissolves.
I scour him with prickly truth but he bristles.

I say *you can find a way.*
Don't say *borrow my hope* anymore.
I say *you are loved,*
say *please don't leave.*

> Then my son walks down the driveway in his black hood,
> bent over, limping, hands curled unnaturally.

He says *there is no help.*
Says *I can't do this.*
Says *I just need one more.*
He doesn't say why. He can't say why.
He says *I'm insane, okay?*

> Then I close the door, maybe for good, throw out bottles, lie on a floor
> to cry, maybe for the last time, scroll through pictures of his daughter.

I can tuck him in my smallest pocket.
Act as if he's a starfish who might regrow.
Believe he's somewhere I can't follow.

> Then the top of my head will stay soft,
> grief will clear until it becomes
> heart, unattached, clean.

While I wait, I look up to see a red bird
flying into a white ending sky.

New York City Police Report #953

[Train operator Karen Daley did see a person
lying in a fetal position on the Northbound
G track 750 feet in the tunnel north of Hoyt St.]

My son, with his broken shoulder, bleeding brain,
is sleeping, a clutch of IV lines snaking
around his fragile body, red for blood,
clear for salt, two for the unholy pain.

[Operator Daley did stop
the train but was unable to come to a complete stop
until all the cars passed over Aided.]

When he wakes, a chicken leg
is on his tray, but he won't let me help,
says: *I'm not a child.*
I'm used to being in hospitals alone.

[No criminality suspected.]

It's different than grief, that blanket of absence
covering me down the years. This time,
it's fear of hope, this time. This time
he'll leave his hospital bed healed.

Remember his light.

Supplication

Oh lord hear our prayers.

Hear those still, unmoaning mounds
under newspapers on frozen streets.

Hear how mothers of broken children,
no matter how lost, keen silently.

Hear each of us whose living skin has been flayed
by betrayal and our own salted tears.

Now lord hear our cries of recognition
as we see you in a flaming leaf's spiral,

incense rising above the coffin like hope,
snow studded with red berries, this bright world.

My Son's Birthday

Who was the first firstborn?
A little squib curlicued
in some mother's belly
until stillborn or earthborn.

You and I are both firstlings,
freeborn at first, then all your born
days took over, turning into borne
nights that have lasted so long,

too long for me to bear.
Today you're in a place
I cannot call, no more
wishes, no happy birth day.

I want such borning
as would be, could be
a different being, born
again into a better body,

but still my body, but not
your same body. Then you,
airborne, would leave me
all the same and again

you would be freeborn,
not in thrall to torment
trailing like an afterbirth.
You'd be still, being born.

Part Three

Author's Note

In 2018 I discovered that the man who raised me was not my biological father. Both men and my mother had died by then. In the following poems, I call the man who raised me and who I thought was my father "second father" or "not-father." My biological father is "first father" or "true father."

How to Be Born Twice

Order 23andme. Forget it when your daughter has a baby.

Remember her infant eyelashes.

Open computer one morning.
Find out you're fifty percent Ashkenazi.
Feel elated. You knew you must be Jewish.

Remember how your father taught you to see a lavender sky.

Realize you might have a different father.
Google Norman Peterzell, the man your mother dated
before she married Grant.
Track down Norman's children and wait for their DNA results.
Receive confirmation they are your half-siblings.

Remember locking yourself in your parents' bedroom
when you babysat for your five brothers and sisters,
who rampaged, half-naked, jumping from the balcony.
Cry now that they're only half-siblings.

Norman was your father. Was.
Feel orphaned all over again.
Understand you'll never know what he knew.

Remember how your parents danced to steel drums.

Unsheltered

In the beginning, birdsmall, I lived in a drawer,
then a tiny brown-shingled house,
finally expansive redwood and glass.
Each home held secrets scattered
like bullets waiting to be deployed,
but I knew where they were, I walked
on pebbled ground into my majority,
carried a few pellets in pockets.
Now one secret unravels into coils
of unanswerable questions. Filled with
wonder, I'm left to live unsheltered.

When they tore down our last house,
was it dismantled one joist at a time,
studs, nails pried out of soft redwood
or did they smash those expansive windows
and skylights as if no one had ever looked
through glass toward an answering sky?
When the great stone fireplace fell to rubble,
did anyone hear its susurration:
Why did you leave? Who was your father?

And the roaring reply from a black beam
that held up home before it collapsed to earth:
I don't know. I don't know.

Undone

If you find out your father was not
your father, do you fall off the family
tree like a red leaf that turns to ground
as if you could unlove all the ancestors
whose name you bear, the grandmother who wrote
you a lullaby, the white-haired aunt who whispered
dreams, the gorgeous uncle who died young?

Where do you put their voices before you
have nothing new to hear? Are they still yours
or must they be undone, unremembered,
your second father's paintings unhung?

Double Helix

I wonder where I live as I fall through

genetics, but the fine cords

between my mother, my son, my daughter,

my sisters and brothers spin into a bright net

holding me high above tundra,

where I can see a lone gentoo penguin,

its red beak angling toward the sky in search

of its own kind, trumpeting its existence.

Incarnations

Last summer I went to a past life
regression weekend, hoping
to discover who I had been.
I didn't know I already knew.

At eight years old, I wept blindly
over the Dutch girl in her attic.
Later, those dreams of Kristallnacht,
flat grey countryside flashing by.

It turned out my father was across the river,
safe from one kind of war at least.
How I've missed him since the test
revealed my Jewish heritage.

He would have taught me
to be radical with attention,
head close to the wind,
to write as if my life depended on it.

I would have listened to his bright soul,
would have led him toward his end,
tenderly rubbing his long feet as one last time
he asked for a poem. I could give that to him.

Origin Story

In the moment of making me, my mother asked my fathers:
Will you crush black-eyed susans into a singing
bowl and make rain fall backward?
Will you scatter clues across the crackled welkin,
fold summer into quilts to lie on every season,
stroking the moon until it flares orange,
while we flaunt our bodies, able to wrest
another succulent day from gods who guard the future?

The first father answered my mother:
I will leave you but always be with my daughter.
Drawing aliveness from a honeycomb of hours,
she will incant *I am here*. I'll help her burnish
words into eyecharms, cover her in tufted vetch
all her mossy days. I'll give her a valley of fire
to carry in her arms. I'll teach her that red-twigged
dogwood is true home.

The second father answered:
I will make the singing bowl and the rain.
I will flood hard dirt until baby's breath grows,
flash red feathers in ragged quince.
I will collect stones from every river for a cairn
to mark our curling toward whatever comes next.
When we breach the distance, we will eat starfruit,
and I will love your daughter.

First Father Speaks

I'll never call you daughter in this life,
I'm a benevolent dybbuk and you're a tummler,
entertaining your audience with a tale
of three parents, weighing who knew
what like a Talmudic scholar.

Might as well kvell over alleles, blue eyes,
the law of independent assortment:
one crinkled brow, a gap in your teeth,
what else? I remain beyond your arms,
out of focus in old photos you can't
smell or hear. You have to conjure me
until I'm more than only half your DNA,
like meeting a stranger you already know.

Second Father Speaks

My squash partner and I are invited to dinner
on Claremont Avenue in Morningside Heights,

where my daughter lives in a five-floor walkup
with a junkie from the suburbs and an intrusion of roaches.

We sit on the floor of a windowless room,
eat cheese fondue from an avocado pot.

Robin is eighteen and thinks she is worldly because
of the gap year when she hitchhiked with a Vietnam vet

to Switzerland. I wanted her to work with Margaret Mead,
but she has a mind of her own. Sometimes I wonder

if she is even mine, her small bones nothing like
my six-foot-three-frame. I've taught her Prokofiev,

osmosis, the Dow, to laugh at my dark funny stories.
When she got pregnant three weeks before graduation,

I held her hand during the procedure.
Now she's scudding away from me

to other men, a husband, a different father.
But tonight she's still my daughter.

Hegira

To step out of your body is to become untethered,
a great push upwards carries you closer and closer

to your fear until just before it's so high
you feel you are dying

    there   is   the   light

and you know you carry your father
with you, arm in arm, though he doesn't realize,

he thinks he's on his own journey
but you call him Daddy to feel safer

and as you transcend even the light
to join a darkness untorn by any glint,

you feel the dark can hold you after all,
as you hold him, cradled in a universe

made serene, you are crowned with stars,
queen of all that matters.

Hecate Incarnate

When my second father died it was too late,
too late for tender words, too late for forgetting
the years of his back turned against me
as he embraced his witchy wife in her dark wig
—oh how she made him soften like wax
to fit her mold while she cackled bitter lies,
twisting our past into a mirror of her madness,
shouting she would stick a knife in my heart
as if I were guilty of *his* sin:
cutting out flesh of his flesh
to join her in their unspeakable bed,
where they fed their fat stories with self-pity
and rage and greed and awful passion
and he believed them all.

Warren

My not-father's wife has made a roast
and mashed potatoes in August.
Meat fills every room, already stuffed
with stacks of records and papers,
an encrusted diving bell, white rocks
from Greece, photographs, books on tape.
My father's artwork covers the dark walls.
A seven-foot golden velvet sofa,
which looked right in expansive
redwood and glass, now barely fits
in what he calls the living room.
The house is hermetic,
as if windows never opened.
~
I bring my father peanut butter
and jam sandwiches at his request.
In the fridge are a dozen jars
of egg yolks, like an experiment
gone bad, and three heads of brown
lettuce he won't let me toss:
She's saving them for the rabbits.
They do not have rabbits.
In a drawer, hundreds of bottle
tops, rubber bands, plastic tabs,
corks. My father can't explain what
they are for *but they're important.*
~
After he's stopped speaking to us
for three years, we find out our father
had died two months before. We drive
to his small street. A dumpster is filled
with rolled up rugs, coffee table legs
sticking straight out of the top.
A demolition crew wearing masks
clears the hoarder's bounty. My father's
paintings are piled six deep in the garage,

the basement, waiting to be dumped.
We take as many as we can fit in our car
to hang in future houses, free to breathe.

Recall

I don't remember when my second father died.
I don't remember if he held my hand
after he drove me to the abortionist's.
I don't remember that he'd kiss me
on the mouth or if he knew I wasn't his.
I don't remember when he stopped painting.
I don't remember that he didn't speak to me for three years.
I don't remember what I felt when he died.
I don't remember what fathers are for.

February 4

If you're born on the same day as your mother,
you lose more than usual when she dies,
as you wonder how to celebrate and mourn.

      Later, walking in a southern country
on a dirt road at your birthday's dawn,

dozens of iridescent, palm-sized morphos
hover around your head, they move forward with you,

their flit and flute stirring deep air until
you are bewildered by happiness,

remembering how your mother would brush
her eyelashes across your cheek, butterfly

kisses she'd say, and for the rest of this life,
you find blue butterflies everywhere,

painted on sidewalks, printed on paper,
so when your granddaughter is born

on that same day, and you sense your mother's hand,
you're surprised only by joy.

Names

She called me to life on her birthday,
so we grew like unnatural twins.
Naming me for a dying uncle,
she branded me with young death.
She called me selfish, asking too much.
When I brought her Old-Fashioneds
on a tray each afternoon, drowsy
with the unsaid, I knew those sweet cherries
were not any kind of reward.
She followed me west as if the country
were a cradle she could rock. Lying down
for the last time, she told me to care
for my sisters and brothers, *her* children.
She never called me by my first father's name.

Chiromancy

We gathered at the continent's edge
as our mother, a white-haired priestess,
breathed toward her bourn.
Under a generous sun, she read our palms,
intent on each child's curved thumb,
map of lines. Heart, life, fate, head,
she gave away what she had left,
or inventoried what she still wanted for us:

You need to toughen up
Turn toward a tower of stones
Build your confidence
Forget any forgotten words for fear
Read between the lines
Take care of fragile memory
Lift above a rough black sea
Let an arrow of geese pierce your grief

Last Spring

When the mist lifts,
Mt. Pisquah is still there,
its wet green flanks waiting
in any weather while my mother
lays down in her own landscape
of soft, folded skin, and she remembers
another mountain she'd like to climb once more,
to be at the summit surveying this unbearably vivid day
before giving birth to the next life.

She doesn't inventory what she's lost,
but we bear witness to what remains,
the way Mt. Pisquah stands irreducible
no matter how many wild iris grow and wither.

Each season is as unique as my mother's face
when she turns with eager eyes toward those
who enter her room, still curious to know
the contours of the hearts she gathers for her journey.
She's packing light, discovering how little she needs after all:
her skin, a bed, her daughters' voices carrying her on.

Call and Response Double Sonnet

Early spring is a time for courage
    Or is it faith?
a time for the brave only
    Were you afraid
to expose tender new buds of growing
    in moist soil
to a raw uncertain season
    as yellow clusters fall off forsythia
undaunted by the risk of death
    the rosebuds might freeze?
at the hand of sudden changes in the weather
    You could gather in daffodils
but sending forth tiny new shoots
    like your many children
irrepressible.
    Was this your mettle?
Daring the cold and the wind
    to wither such greening
and seeking the sun
    as if a father
they only will survive to find fulfillment
    as if a mother
in a gentler time
    has covered earth with her own body
brave enough to dare
    waiting for another season
to draw life from strong roots
    to give back a multitude of mothers.

                              Dorothy Nelson Dellabough, 1959
                              Robin Dellabough, 2020

Water Lilies

Rushing through a maze stuffed

with Gaugins, Van Goghs,

I try not to look, no time, too thirsty,

where is water? Where is the café?

Accidentally dead end in front of Monet's triptych,

a small room without windows but filled with reflection.

I know that my mother stood here

more than sixty years ago,

while my true father sulked in a bar.

As she gazed at the painting,

my not-father came up to her,

asked if he knew her and she recognized him

from the street they both grew up on.

I can't ask her when she saw him next.

I can't ask if she knew I'd stand

sixty years later in front of the mystery

even beauty cannot answer.

The Dog Eats A Letter From My Mother When I Was 18

loving
        loaded

with his denouement
back home
        will mean burning

emerging is a real gut
all the humanity
        whether or not

he seems so
schedule

man dismissed
        remarks
         monotone
         questions
see that the same

at understanding
tedious defining

afraid to go
suffer from
and dip into

east always view
feels about
understand

without even realizing
        introduced
        asked for
your activities

amazement
my money

a young girl who knew

the ride

troubles getting into
(intellectually)
his kind of person

a trip
now, big mustache
some exploration
        relatively
late late show
        acceptance of

sounds fabulous
on T. S. Eliot–our mutual disappointment
part of the new me
I rejoice to say I am not worried

so long as you can believe in yourself come what may
a corny way to put it

could be push
back where you
       (you know)
to recapture
wild mix thrown in

Rigging

Each morning our mother gathered us
around the marriage bed that hung
on ropes and pulleys from the living room
ceiling, our father's solution to a small house.
Together we'd push it back up for the day.
Though we lived nowhere near the sea,
fishnet and seaglass trimmed the bottom
as if our parents were on an island honeymoon.
Did they feel like voyagers during their brief nights,
sailing away from a tribe of children?
Did they crave a trill of sandpipers
leading them toward the edge of sleep?
A gutter of seagulls dropped feathers the children
couldn't catch until all were safe in the floating bed.

Making Sense

It begins with my father, already dead,
but still vivid in his height and heft,
black hair turned white. I can hear
his deep voice droning on til he is talking
to my mother, also dead, maybe telling
her he's sorry for his monologues and mistakes
or maybe he just loved the sound of his words.
My mother loved to eat tongue,
corn fritters, and caviar. She also liked the taste
of Old-Fashioneds, which I would make
and bring to her on a tray. Sixty years later,
I can smell the sick sweetness of maraschino
cherries or was it the whiskey?
She managed to scratch our backs every night,
calming all six of us into quiet, if not sleep.
I can still feel her tender hands, and I forgive her.

Before and After Kennedy

I drove to Jones Beach, with its Art Deco
welcome sign. Near the ocean's edge,
brimming with green and white waves,
the flawless shore was stippled
with skittering sandpipers, plump black-backed gulls.
I thought of my black-haired mother here,
surrounded by her brood sticky with ice cream
and sand, before this beach was crowded,
before Kennedy was killed, before
the brewing future became bittersweet.

After Kennedy, we were still young
and smooth-skinned, golden songs
of love or peace played nonstop
as everything billowed
into an unending summer night,
each moment fraught with new,
the scent of Jean Nate, Coppertone, Mateus,
the utter innocence of first sex—oh!
now I remember as if I never knew,
we were pregnant, me at seventeen,
my mother at forty-two. I went to a secret
office on Duck Pond Road, while she lost
her baby on a Caribbean beach,
the opposite of innocence.

Affliction (3)

The year I was afflicted with genetics
opened like nesting boxes, a stuck puzzle.
First that I am Ashkenazi,
my seven siblings only halves,
that my father was not my father,
but a man who lived and died in Florida.
The smallest box, the heart, was left unopened:
Did my mother know? After the affliction,
I turned my back on secrecy, toward gifts
my fathers gave me—how to look at trees,
to shape words sharply, to hear music beyond
clichés, to swing fearlessly across water,
even if no one was on the other side,
proud and alive, a lovely doubleness.

Exposure

In the photographs where one father disappears,
he leaves a blank space where another comes into view.

I go back and back to before birth, before the hard choosing,
an impossible choice even for a witch or an angel.

My mother was no angel. Those who thought her saintlike
to bear six children in eight years didn't know about her

breakdown, the pills, drinking. Still, she hasn't faded
from any pictures, she's vivid in her grey-haired glory,

mouth open in hilarity, eyes glinting with secret mirth.
Even for her, my parentage was a secret. I'll keep looking

at those changeling images until it's my daughter's turn
to study them and remember me, how I loved her.

I Find A Haiku Written 36 Years Before My DNA Test

Father of my years,
you died before our talking.
But it was a dream.

Affliction (4)

The year I was afflicted with air,
pushing through recovered memory,
I found breath in the strangest place:
flat, plain desert rocks painted red,
that made my birth wholly possible.

I fought to claim my right to air,
without any belief in memory
except a glimpse of blood so red
I didn't know if I was in a place
of welcome, or a forbidding place.

Filled with the struggle to separate
from a rising above air I made origami
memory out of parents who were possible,
not a father who was as impossible
as stone bones holding me in place.

I do not want to fight with genetics.
Let me claim my days, cloaked in red,
find a heart-shaped rock on a red
beach to conjure whatever's possible
in the same familiar air.

I will grow into my tomorrows
as red as a cheek kissed in battle
when such a thing was not possible
yet happened in a place ruled by
hard-earned, capacious air.

Collaboration

A jet cuts through fog like a prehistoric bird
with beady red eyes flashing its descent.
Red blinking lights next door. The young boy,
who dances in silence, has threatened his grandmother
with words or blood. My own son talks
of playground wounds, how he tries to walk
away, the taunts reducing him to tears.

I put a dark red candle on the sill, sit
with little ceremony. The candle melts unevenly.
The flame blurs into gold, and the gold seems to speak:

Where do you live?
In dreams of endless grey camps, men and women
without names or faces, silently sweeping.
Where do you live?
In the future, fifty years.
Where do you live?
In California, far from there. Now earth shakes,
confirming one reality.

~

I was a young Quaker mother when I wrote
those lines thirty years ago. Today I'm a grandmother.
I think of the boy they tried to pull
to safety through a hole in the shameful wall,
while on the other side they broke his back.

Even this year in our capital a new mob
dressed in furs and flags, shirts emblazoned
with *Camp Auschwitz*, broke glass
as viciously as Kristallnacht.
At least now I know why I dreamed those grey dreams,
remember that boy: I'm half Ashkenazi.

Where do you live?
In New York on Maple Street,
in the endless mystery of violence,

of blood. I will light a candle tonight
for both my Christian Scientist father
and my Jewish father, for everyone who's died
from the obscenity of ignorance.

1989/2021

Family Dinner, 1976

Everyone is still alive, talking about death.
My not-father says the first thing
we should see every morning is a skull.

My mother announces to the table
that Robin's always been afraid
of dying by twenty-four.

My father asks my age now.
Twenty-four. It feels like a plague.
He reminds me to guard against eagles

that prey upon babies, his black way
of teaching me to be fearless.
I can hear how I listen to him,

my laugh the same for forty years
in this fearless after-life: Grant
telling me he is my true father.

Acknowledgments

The following poems appeared previously in these publications:
The Eighth Year *(Maryland Poetry Review)*
Hegira *(Blue Unicorn)*
Instructions for Letting Go of a Marriage *(Persimmon Tree)*
Last Spring *(Lines + Stars)*
My Boy *(One Sentence Poems)*
Supplication *(Westchester Review)*
Undone *(Halfway Down the Stairs)*
The Velocity of Nostalgia *(Stoneboat Literary Journal)*
What's the Worst That Can Happen? *(Westchester Review)*
Furtive Hours *(Right Hand Pointing)*
Dwelling *(Right Hand Pointing)*
File Cabinet *(Halfway Down the Stairs)*
Natural History: Apis mellifera *(Meow Meow Pow Pow)*
The Dog Eats A Letter From My Mother When I Was 18 *(Tiny Spoons)*
How I Say God *(Friends Journal)*

Thanks to all my teachers who helped me find my voice, including Suzanne Cleary, Alex Dimitrov, Amy Holman.

To my workshop friends, who provided such thoughtful feedback for many of the poems in this volume: Eric Odynocki, Michael Quattrone, M.A. Scott.

To my MOI group for unconditional creative cheerleading: Deb Fields, Betty Ming Liu, Zoee Luna, Kathleen McCarthy, Lea Richardson, Karen Viola.

To my newly discovered Peterzell family for so graciously and generously welcoming me as their sister: Sarah Peterzell Barry and James Peterzell.

To my Dellabough siblings for ceaseless love and support through the years: Liana, Kassia, Damien, Derek, with special thanks to Marlitt, who designed the cover of my dreams.

Finally, thanks to Joel, whose courage is humbling, and to Flynn, my daughter in words and in heart.

Robin Dellabough is a poet, editor, and writer with a master's degree from UC Berkeley School of Journalism. Her poems have appeared in *Stoneboat, Fifth Estate, Lines + Stars, Halfway Down the Stairs, The Gentian Journal, Tiny Spoon, Maryland Poetry Review, Blue Unicorn, Negative Capability, Gargoyle, Westchester Review, Friends Journal,* and other publications and anthologies. A founding partner at Lark Productions: A Book Company, she has written, edited and contributed to more than sixty books, including *The Poets' Corner* by John Lithgow. Her current position is Projects Director, Publishers Marketplace/Publishers Lunch.